Mountain Bike
Repair and Maintenance

W. Lindorf

Mountain Bike
Repair and Maintenance

WARD LOCK

A WARD LOCK BOOK
First published in the UK 1995
by Ward Lock
Wellington House
125 Strand
LONDON WC2R 0BB

A Cassell Imprint

Translation from the German by Andrew Wilson in association with
First Edition Translations Ltd, Cambridge, UK

Distributed in the United States by Sterling Publishing Co., Inc.
387 Park Avenue South, New York, NY 10016-8810

Distributed in Australia by Capricorn Link (Australia) Pty Ltd
2/13 Carrington Road, Castle Hill, NSW 2154

A British Library Cataloguing in Publication Data block for this book may be
obtained from the British Library.

ISBN 0 7063 7420 7
Typeset by Computech, Cheshire, in association with
First Edition Translations Ltd, Cambridge, UK

Consultant: Tim Woodcock

Contents

The mountain bike

No other single design has influenced the bicycle market as much as the mountain bike. The new technology, such as indexed gears, efficient cantilever brakes and comfortable suspension systems, is becoming increasingly accepted. But despite this new technology, all the working parts are still accessible, and it's great fun to maintain and repair your bike yourself.

With a modicum of mechanical skill, patience and the right tools, you can remedy any faults that might arise on your mountain bike without having to take it to a mechanic every time something goes wrong.

As you tinker with your bike, you might discover you have a real mechanical aptitude and decide to set up a well-equipped workshop of your own. Care and maintenance are important if the brakes and transmission are to remain in good working order and you are to get as much fun as possible from your bike. If you check your mountain bike regularly and become familiar with the various components, you will be spared nasty surprises when you take it for a spin. A well-maintained bike with components in good working order will go a long way to making touring and commuting accident free. The quality and value of your mountain bike will be maintained in the long term.

The development of the mountain bike

The mountain bike phenomenon has its roots in the antics of a couple of innovative cycle fanatics from California. In 1975, Gary Fisher and Charles Kelly were tearing down dirt tracks on Mount Tamalpais, a mountain near San Francisco, on their old "bombers". "Bombers" are bicycles with thick balloon tyres and a curved frame, the kind used by paperboys in old American films. Fisher and Kelly found their private races on unpaved roads so enjoyable that they began modifying their fat tyre bikes to make them even more stable and safe.

Eventually, they had a special design produced by a framebuilder friend of theirs by the name of Joe Breeze; they fitted the frame with cantilever brakes and five-speed derailleur gears. The first

The robust, tightly sealed transmission system of the bike withstands extreme stresses. The stiff frame means that more power is transmitted with every turn of the pedals.

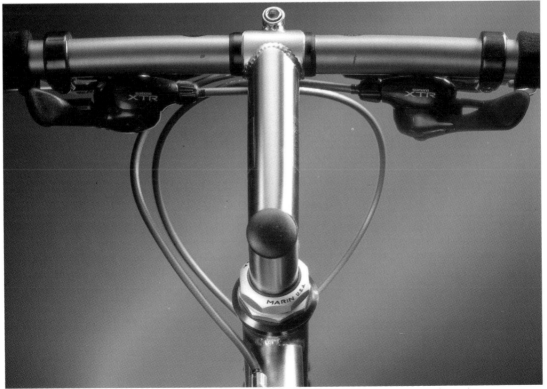

Easily operated shifters, ergonomically positioned under the handlebars, and sophisticated indexed shifting systems offer greater convenience and comfort.

With quick-release hubs, a wheel can be removed in just a few seconds. High-quality sealed hubs will keep running smoothly for long periods.

Elegant and practical: modern materials make a mountain bike as robust yet light as possible.

mountain bike was born. Soon friends were expressing an interest in buying the bikes, so Breeze had to produce more frames. The mountain bike spread all over America and then inundated Europe. About 70 per cent of all bikes sold in the world market are now mountain bikes.

Materials

The first bikes had steel frames; since then, a whole range of different materials has been used, including aluminium and steel alloys, carbon, titanium and even exotic metals such as beryllium and boralyn. Whatever the material, the aim remains the same: to produce a bike that is as light and stable as possible. The most commonly used materials are steel and aluminium, which are also reasonably priced. Both have long been used in frame building and can be worked relatively simply and safely.

All bicycles, including mountain bikes of course, consist of a frame and components. The components are the parts such as gears, brakes, bearings and wheels that are bolted on to the frame. And it is these parts that you can service and repair yourself. All you need to do this, in addition to the right tools, are a little skill and patience and the tips and instructions given in this book.

Maintenance and repairs

A new mountain bike is quite an investment. In order to keep all the parts functioning smoothly and to maintain the bike's value over many years, t is advisable to maintain and repair it regularly, as you would a car. Because a mountain bike idden in open country is exposed to much greater stresses and shocks than a racing or road ike, certain parts of a mountain bike require greater care and maintenance than those on other bikes. Mud, grime and damp attack bearings and gears. Impacts loosen spokes, screws, bolts and headsets. Jumps and steep climbs and descents place a great deal of stress on the bottom bracket and the whole transmission system. And after a fall, the bike should of course be checked over thoroughly. Because of the much greater demands made of mountain bikes, many of their components are much better built and more durable than those fitted to other types of bicycle.

Regular inspections

Expensive designs they may be, but all the components on a mountain bike are still relatively simple to look over and take apart. It is important that you should use the right tools for repairs, otherwise disappointments are bound to occur. Basically you should check your bike over regularly, inspect certain parts and clean everything properly in order to extend the bike's life. Constant exposure to dampness will rust even the best components, so that eventually their performance deteriorates or they fail altogether. Bearings like those in the hubs or the bottom bracket can be destroyed by dirt and rough surfaces and should therefore be serviced regularly. These checks take up very little time. At the same time, you will get to know your bicycle

much better and become increasingly proficient at adjusting and reassembling components – an advantage in an emergency when you are in open country. Good maintenance also saves on expensive repairs and helps to protect you from unpleasant surprises on your next outing, when you might be miles away from the nearest telephone box.

Maintenance simply means disassembling certain moving parts, cleaning and coating them with grease or some other lubricant in order to protect and keep them moving and then reassembling them. On mountain bikes, these moving parts are mainly bearings: in the hubs, the bottom bracket, the headset and the pedals. They also include all other moving parts: chain, seat pillar, gear shifters and brakes, as well as the cables that control gears and brakes. Only a dirt-

There is no mystery about adjusting the gears correctly. If the transmission system is rattling, repairs can often be done quickly and simply.

encrusted, unoiled cable can significantly impair the operation of modern indexed gear changers. Cable maintenance takes only a few minutes and consists of putting a few drops of lubricant in the right place. That's all it takes to have everything running smoothly.

Checking and adjusting

Brakes that slip and squeal are not only a nuisance but positively dangerous. Constant wear and tear on the brake blocks makes it necessary to adjust cantilever brakes from time to time. If the brake blocks are too worn, there is no alternative but to replace them. All these operations take only a few minutes, but the benefits are enormous, not only for your enjoyment of cycling but also for your safety.

One extremely important point is the inspection of the bike's entire steering system: handlebars, stem and headset. All connections must be absolutely secure, there should be no play at all in the handlebars. So check the bolts on the stem at regular intervals. It is equally important to ensure that the headset is properly adjusted. It should not be tightened up too much, since this will make the bicycle impossible to steer and could lead to some unpleasant surprises in open country.

On the other hand, the headset should not have too much play in it either, i.e. should not be too loose, otherwise the bearing races will be knocked out of alignment, the ball bearings will be damaged and you will have to buy a new headset. Dirt penetrating the headset also grinds down the ball bearings and the smooth surfaces of the races and slowly but surely damages the headset beyond repair. So disassemble it regularly in order to clean the bearings and repack them in grease.

The same rule applies to all other bearings (hubs, pedals and bottom bracket). The bolts connecting the cranks to the bottom bracket axle must be tightly fastened. If they are not, there will be a loud click from the pedals as you push them round. If the fault is not remedied in time, the

In order to avoid nasty surprises, always make sure both tyres are correctly inflated before taking your bike out for a ride.

The bottom bracket should be inspected and serviced once or twice a year. Modern fully-sealed bearings, on the other hand, are maintenance-free.

Check that the cantilever brakes are correctly adjusted before every ride, in order to protect yourself and your bike from damage.

bearings will be knocked out of alignment and become unusable. Wheel hubs and pedals should also be dismantled and serviced from time to time.

If there is a constant rattling from the transmission system, then the gear changing mechanism is at fault. Any incorrect adjustment will usually be noticed immediately: the chain will either not move at all or only with difficulty from cog to cog. However, even worse things can happen: sometimes the chain slides off the front or rear cogs and becomes jammed between the gear system and the frame. This is a potential cause of some fairly nasty accidents. In such cases, or if it is excessively worn, the chain will have to be replaced. With the right tools and a little skill even this should be no problem.

Their thick, knobbly tyres and strong rims will take mountain bikes safely over rough country. And yet trouble sometimes strikes, even with a cross-country bike. Fortunately, a buckled wheel is not as bad as it might seem. A few turns with a spoke key and the wheel will be running true again. Flat tyres are fairly common, even with mountain bikes. Professional racing cyclists can change an inner tube in two minutes. There is no need for you to be as quick as that, but a few little tips will make it easier to get the tyre on and off the rim.

So don't panic: everything touched upon briefly here is described in greater detail in the relevant chapter. All the jobs and the equipment you require will be explained as you read on.

The cockpit control panel: handlebar-mounted brake levers and gear shifters provide easy access to all the bike's controls.

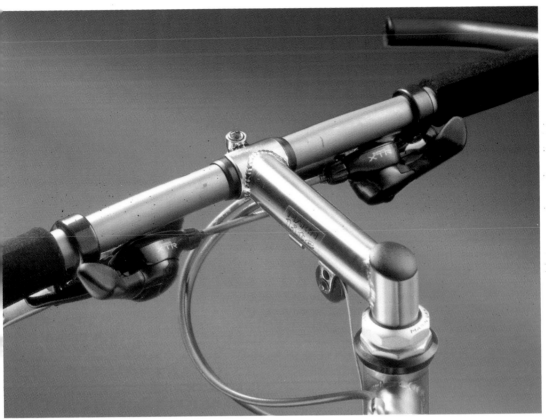

The gear cables on a modern mountain bike need regular servicing in order to keep gear shifting as smooth and efficient as possible.

Thick, knobbly tyres provide good damping and much-needed traction on all surfaces, while sturdy rims offer comfort and safety.

Maintenance routines

Before each trip you should check the following components and answer the questions for each one:

Brakes
Are the brake blocks positioned correctly?
Are the brake blocks worn?
Are the blocks dragging on the rim?
Are the brake cables properly positioned and connected?

Headset
Is the bike easy to steer?
Is there excess play?

Stem
Is it firmly tightened, or can it be twisted?

Handlebars
Are they firmly tightened?

Wheels
Are the quick-release levers properly tightened?

Tyres
Is there enough tread, and are they properly pumped up?
Are there any foreign bodies embedded in the tyre walls?

Annual service:

Bottom bracket
Disassemble, clean and grease ball bearings.

Hubs
Disassemble, clean and grease ball bearings.

The following checks should be carried out every three months:

Bottom bracket
Is there any lateral play on the cranks?
(Readjust if necessary!)

Chain
How worn is it? Is it too dry?
(Lubricate, or if necessary replace.)

Wheels
Is there any lateral or vertical movement?
(Correct if necessary.)

Gears
Are they correctly adjusted?
(Clean and lubricate cables, replace if necessary.)

Hubs
Are they running smoothly and silently?
(Adjust if necessary.)

Brakes
Do they grip well? Is the caliper action properly centred?
(Adjust, replace blocks if necessary. If they are not operating smoothly, lubricate cables and cantilever bodies.)

Headset
Disassemble, clean and grease ball bearings.

Pedals
Disassemble, clean and grease ball bearings.

Tools

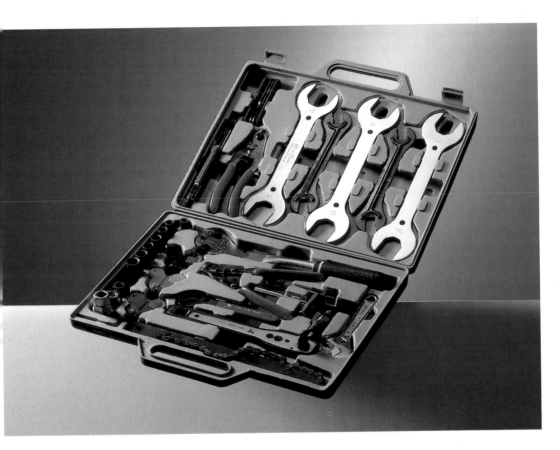

The key to success is having the right tools for the job. With the help of a simple basic tool kit, you will be able to strip down and repair your bike at home.

Even the best mechanic will get nowhere with the wrong spanner. Before starting repair or maintenance work on a wheel, you should check that you have the right tools for the job. There is nothing more frustrating than beginning a job and coming to a standstill right in the middle of it, because you cannot undo a bolt. Although it has around 2,000 separate parts, a mountain bike is relatively simply constructed and only a small number of specialist tools are required. That's the beauty of doing your own bicycle repairs: a great deal can be achieved with just minimal outlay.

A basic tool kit

A basic tool kit, most of which is certainly already available in virtually every home, would include screwdrivers (flat-blade and cross-head), a complete set of combination spanners and Allen keys, a pair of combination pliers and a pair of long-nose pliers. A rubber mallet is sometimes useful for loosening jammed parts. The bike-specific tools you will require include a pair of cable cutters, a spoke key, a chain tool, two tyre levers and a puncture repair kit. These tools are not expensive. You will need them for jobs such as changing cables and replacing or repairing chains. It is also a simple matter to make temporary adjustments to the wheels if they are running out of true, or to patch up an inner tube in the event of a puncture.

a suitable lockring and peg spanner. Even the 32 mm or 36 mm spanners you will need for the headset are not to be found in a standard tool kit.

If you want to fit a new freewheel and sprockets to the rear wheel, you will have to have an appropriate freewheel remover and a chain whip. Special cone spanners are needed to open up front and rear hubs in order to get at the insides. Dedicated DIY mechanics would be well advised to acquire a suitable workstand. There are various types, some freestanding, some for mounting on a wall or workbench, but all of them hold the bike in position while you work on it from all sides. And by acquiring a wheel stand as well, you will be able to true even badly buckled wheels.

Specialist tools

If you wish to service your bike regularly yourself and keep it in good shape, you will have to dig a little deeper into your pocket. In order to be able to service the various sets of bearings or the different parts of a wheel, you will need to acquire specialist tools; the sizes you require will depend on the particular bike you have. In order to disassemble the bottom bracket bearing, for example, you will need a crank extractor and

Trail tool kit

Anybody buying their first mountain bike should also purchase a trail tool kit at the same time. It is traditionally carried in a saddlebag. Small, light combination tools usually incorporate screwdrivers, the necessary Allen keys and sometimes even the indispensable chain breaker. A handy spoke key, two tyre levers and a puncture repair outfit complete the trail kit. Emergency spares, such as cables and a roll of tape, will also fit into

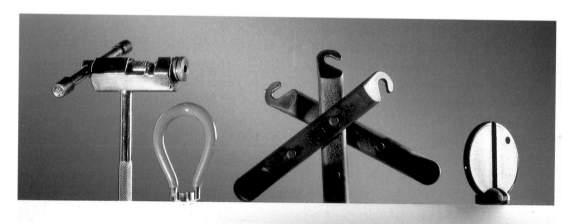

Essential items in any emergency tool kit: a compact chain tool, spoke keys in the correct sizes and tyre levers.

A workstand makes working on a mountain bike much easier. It will hold the bike at the correct working height and is adjustable in all directions.

Cone spanners are needed for all adjustable bearings, such as hubs. Thin cone spanners are available in various sizes.

Tools are reasonably priced. DIY mechanics will need this freewheel remover and chain whip for dismantling sprocket clusters.

A whole range of specially formulated cleaning and lubrication products for each part of your bike is now available from a variety of different manufacturers.

a saddlebag. You won't be able to fix everything, but the tool kit will be sufficient to cope with the commonest causes of breakdowns when out on a ride. (It's also worth carrying some small change or a phonecard, so that you can call friends to help out if all else fails.)

Cleaning and lubrication materials

The old standbys of sewing machine oil and ben-zine have now been replaced by a whole range of different cleaning and lubricating products for bicycles. These products are milder and often biodegradable. To clean your bike, use a special cold cleaner for bikes and then wash it off with water and a brush or sponge. A jet-spray hose will help if your bike is very heavily mud-encrusted, but be careful: never spray water directly at close range at sensitive bearings, such as the headset or chainset, otherwise water may force its way through the seals.

The basic rule is that you should use different products for different parts of the bike and avoid using all-purpose grease. Use grease and lubri-

cants sparingly. For the chain, a thick oil is appro-priate, while a lubricant with synthetic ingredi-ents, such as Teflon, should be used for all cables and moving parts in the gear system. For screw threads or connections between metal parts (pedals, seat posts, bolts on chain or sprocket wheels, etc.), it is best to use specially formu-lated grease. Special bearing grease is also avail-able; it adheres well and repels water.

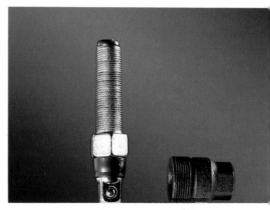

The only correct way of getting at the bottom bracket is with a crank extractor. A tool like this will fit all common types of crank.

Tools for the home workshop

Screwdrivers (flat-blade and cross-head)

Rubber mallet

1 set of combination spanners

1 set of Allen keys

Long-nose pliers

Combination pliers

Spoke key

Chain breaker

Tyre levers

Puncture repair kit

Cable cutter

Headset spanners

Cone spanners

Lockring, pin and peg spanners

Crank extractor

Freewheel remover

Chain whip

Wheel stand

Workstand

Trail tool kit

Multi-tool (Allen keys, screwdrivers)

Chain breaker (if not included in multi-tool)

Tyre levers

Puncture repair kit

10 mm spanner

Spoke key

Pump

Adhesive tape

Spare cables

Brakes

Cantilever brakes have real bite: they grip so well they bring the bike to a halt in seconds. If the rubber blocks squeal or rub, this usually means they are incorrectly adjusted. Two spanners are all you need to adjust them.

The brakes on mountain bikes are some of the simplest but at the same time most important parts on any bike. Professional racing cyclists speeding along at over 80 kph (50 mph) still rely on their cantilever brakes to slow them down. The powerful leverage exerted by cantilever brakes means that the rim is gripped between the blocks as if by forceps. Inexperienced mountain bike riders are often so surprised by the power of the front brake that they are almost catapulted headfirst over the handlebars. If the front brake is applied too vigorously, the front

wheel may even lock, leaving the rider standing on the pedals or, if he is descending a steep incline, bringing the rear wheel up somewhat more sharply than is comfortable.

For this reason, the front brake lever on most mountain bikes is mounted in the factory on the left-hand side of the handlebars. The majority of the population is right-handed.Most people who are startled or needing to brake quickly for some other reason instinctively pull hard on the right-hand lever. If the rear wheel skids along the ground, nothing much will happen. However, if the front wheel locks, the consequences could be unpleasant. The levers on British cycles are arranged differently: the brake lever for the front wheel is mounted on the right-hand side, with the back brake lever on the left.

The correct adjustment

The cycle dealer should have adjusted the cantilever brakes for optimum performance in his workshop. Check them over anyway. New cables often stretch with use, and after a few days' riding in open country the cantilever bodies will be too far away from the rim. A turn on the barrel adjuster on the brake lever is enough to correct this.

Unscrewing the barrel adjuster will shorten the inner cable and the blocks will move closer to the rim. You can also vary the amount of slack in the cables in the same way to suit your own taste. However, you should not be able to pull the lever right up against the handlebars. If you can, the cable is too slack.

If the braking action starts to become less powerful after a few hundred miles and the brake levers have too much travel in them, then the blocks have probably worn and are no longer pressing accurately against the wheel rim when activated. The brakes usually start to squeal and rub as well, particularly when the rims are wet. This is a sure sign that the brake blocks need further adjustment.

This is a warning that should not be ignored: incorrectly adjusted blocks not only considerably reduce braking performance and make irritating noises, they can even end up fouling the spokes and causing a nasty crash. So check the adjustment of your brake blocks regularly, particularly if they are squealing. In fact, squealing brakes are so irritating that you won't need any further prompting to get your tool kit out!

The brake block should sit one to two millimetres (about ⅛ in) below the upper edge of the rim and parallel to it. When the brakes are operated it should not touch the tyre.

Centring the brakes

The design of cantilever brakes, with their two independently mounted cantilever bodies, makes servicing and adjustment easier. The cable runs from the brake lever through the guides fitted to the frame down to the straddle yoke.

The tension on cantilever brakes should be distributed equally between the two cantilever bodies, with the straddle yoke as low as possible over the tyres. The cantilever bodies will then press evenly against the rim and exert maximum power on the wheel. The length of the straddle wire on modern cantilever brakes, and therefore the position of the straddle yoke, is fixed by the manufacturer. On most systems, a short link wire runs from the right-hand cantilever to the yoke, where it is held in place by a nipple; the main brake cable runs through the left-hand side

The tension on cantilever brakes should be distributed equally between the two brake arms, so that the brakes can be properly adjusted to press evenly against the rim.

of the yoke to the left-hand cantilever, where it is fixed by either an Allen key screw or a 10 mm hexagonal nut.

Adjusting the brake blocks

In order to adjust the brake blocks, you will need a 5 mm Allen key and a 10 mm spanner. Holding the block in place with the Allen key, loosen each block locknut with the spanner. You will now be able to move the blocks. They are mounted on the cantilever body on a dished washer, which makes them freely adjustable laterally. There is also scope for limited vertical adjustment.

The blocks should now be positioned relative to the wheel rim so that, when viewed from the side, they lie parallel to it. They must not protrude either above or below the rim. If they are positioned too high, the blocks may dig into the tyre. If they are positioned too low, they can slip off the rim and foul the spokes. Viewed from above or below and looking towards the direction of travel, the front of the block should be closer to the rim than the back. This "toe-in" ensures that when the brakes are activated the front of the block will hit the rim just before the back, thereby strengthening the braking action. This will also prevent the brakes from squealing so irritatingly.

Since 1993, many manufacturers have been moulding small pins on the rear edge of their brake blocks so that they can be correctly positioned relative to the rim when first mounted. These small pins, which are quickly worn away in use, ensure that new brake blocks are held at exactly the right angle to the rim when they are being fitted.

Both blocks should be an equal distance from the cantilever body. In order to check this, most block mounting posts have setting lines engraved on them. Adjust the blocks so that they sit two or three millimetres (1/8 to 3/16 in) away from the rim when at rest. This distance can also be altered by means of the barrel adjuster, which should be slackened off a few turns prior to the final adjustment. This will let out a small amount

Hold the brake block in place from the front with an Allen key, loosen the 10 mm nut with a spanner and adjust the block.

of cable and make it possible to reduce or increase the gap between the cantilever body and the rim.

When the brake block is positioned relative to the rim as described, hold it in position with a 5 mm Allen key and tighten up the locknut. Make sure that the block does not move as you tighten up the locknut.

When the blocks on both sides are correctly adjusted, pull on the brake levers and check the position of the blocks when pressed directly against the rim. If the cantilevers are moving unevenly against the rim, many designs of brake can be easily centred by means of a spring embedded in one of the cantilever bodies. The adjusting screw is located on the side of the cantilever body and can be turned with either a flat-blade screwdriver or an Allen key. If the screw is turned in a clockwise direction, the cantilever body in which the screw is located will move outwards, and vice versa. The spring embedded in the cantilever body reacts to very small movements of the screw. So always adjust the screw by just half a turn at most and then check the effect by pulling on the brake lever and observing the movement of the two cantilever bodies. Both blocks should hit the rim at the same time in order to give optimum performance.

If your brakes are still squealing and rubbing despite having new, correctly adjusted blocks, clean the wheel rims with benzine or a specialist bike cleaner. If the brake blocks have not been renewed, use sandpaper to smooth the hard contact area, which might also be the cause of the squealing. Regular cleaning and lubrication of the

The barrel adjuster on the brake lever controls the gap between the brake blocks and the rim. Unscrewing the adjuster will pull the blocks closer to the rim.

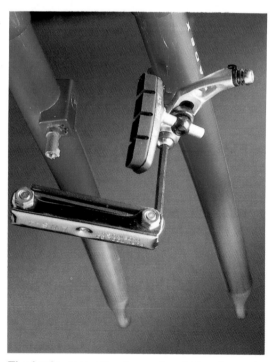

The brake mounting boss should be cleaned and greased once or twice a year. To do this, slacken the brake cable and remove the cantilever body.

cables should also be part of your brake maintenance routine. To do this, untension the brakes and remove the cables from the levers. The cable inners can then be wiped with a cloth dampened with a little cleaning fluid; finally, fill the cable outers with lubricant, such as Teflon or something similar. This will help to reduce friction in the cables, which can have an adverse effect on the brakes' performance.

Excessively long cables waste power. The cables should be arranged neatly in arcs, without kinks; the shortest route is the best. If you want to shorten a cable, disassemble it completely by removing it from the right-hand cantilever (unscrew the Allen key screw or hexagonal nut). Then cut the cable housing to the correct length with cable cutters and replace the cable. Make sure the brakes are properly centred, as described above.

Cleaning the brake mounting bosses

If you ride your bike often over muddy ground or offroad in wet weather, you should also dismantle the cantilever bodies from time to time in order to clean and grease the brake bosses. Use a 5 mm Allen key to loosen the pivot mounting bolts. The return spring is mounted on the brake boss, with a protective cap on the fork side. When reassembling the brakes, make sure that the end of the spring is replaced in the correct hole (usually the middle one) on the brake boss. The other two holes allow you to adjust the spring tension.

Do you want to fine-tune your cantilever brakes? To do this, you can fit various types of brake blocks and discover the best combination for your particular rims. Some block-rim combinations perform better in cold or wet conditions than others. An additional plate designed to tie the pivots together above the brake bolts, known as a brake booster, noticeably stiffens the forks or seat stays and usually gives the brakes added "bite". High-performance brake boosters are very rigid and weigh only a few grams (ounces).

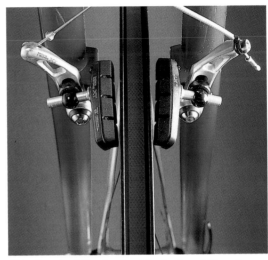

The front of the brake block should be closer to the rim than the back; when at rest, the blocks should sit about two to three millimetres ($^1/_8$ to $^3/_{16}$ in) away from the rim.

The headset

Between the handlebars and the front wheel of a mountain bike is an inconspicuous but important component: the headset. This is a heavy-duty bearing that has to tolerate or absorb any amount of mechanical stress; for this reason, it should be regularly inspected and serviced.

Checking the headset takes literally only a few seconds, so you can do it every time you take your bike out for a ride. Engage the front brake, then with both hands on the handlebars push the bike back and forth. If you notice any play (a slight wobble) in the handlebars, the headset is loose and requires adjustment.

Like any other bearing, the headset needs enough slack for the steerer tube to turn smoothly

with no tight spots. However, there should not be too much play, in order to prevent the bearings going out of alignment and being damaged. The headsets on mountain bikes contain ball or needle bearings. A layer of grease protects the moving parts against dirt and damp while at the same time reducing friction.

The headset absorbs every blow that the front wheel receives. This is why the headset on a mountain bike that takes a lot of battering comes loose much more often than that on a racing or commuting bicycle. As a result, manufacturers and designers have developed various new models and tested them extensively under typical riding conditions in order to make a headset that is as robust and hardy as possible.

The "standard" headset

A "standard" headset is adjusted by loosening or tightening two large hexagonal nuts (usually 32 mm). As with hubs or bottom brackets, the lower one is used to vary the amount of slack while the upper one acts as a locknut. On early mountain bikes, and on other types of bicycle, the head tube has a diameter of one inch (25.4 mm). In order to make frames more stable, Gary Fisher introduced tubes of larger diameter, which in turn required larger headsets. In the American system, these tubes have a diameter of 1¼ in (31.75 mm). Other manufacturers reduced this later to 1⅛ in (28.6 mm), so that there are now three standard sizes in frame building. Equip yourself with the right headset spanners for your bike. It is advisable to take your bike with you when you go to buy tools. In that way, you won't have any unpleasant surprises when you get home.

How to adjust the headset: hold the lower nut in place with a headset spanner and loosen the upper locknut. Then adjust the play in the lower bearings with the lower nut, tighten it up and finally secure the upper locknut.

Adjusting the headset

In order to adjust a loose headset, tighten the lower nut a little (by turning it clockwise) and then test for slack again by engaging the front brake and pushing the handlebars back and forth with both hands. Then continue to tighten the lower hexagonal nut in quarter-turns until there is no more wobbling in the handlebars.

The next check is intended to show whether the headset still has enough play in it to turn smoothly. Lift the bike up by the frame so that the front wheel can move freely. If you line the front wheel up in a straight line with the frame and let go of the handlebars, the wheel will turn to one side or the other of its own accord. If it does not, then the headset is too tight and you will have to loosen off the bottom nut a little.

If both tests show that the headset is correctly adjusted (no detectable wobbling, turns smoothly), hold the lower nut in place with a spanner and tighten the locknut with the second spanner (turning it clockwise), making sure that the lower nut does not move.

Adjusting the Aheadset system: first slacken off the Allen key bolts in the side of the stem, then tighten the bolt running through the cap on the top of the stem (turn it clockwise). Now pull on the front brake and push the handlebars back and forth. If there is no more wobbling in the headset, tighten up the stem.

If the steering is very heavy or the headset cannot be adjusted any further, it will have to be dismantled and serviced or replaced. Any roughness or grinding is a sure sign that dirt and foreign bodies have got into the bearings.

Disassembling the headset

In order to disassemble the headset, first remove the stem, which fits inside the steerer tube of the forks and is fixed by means of a bolt and expander wedge. To do this, just loosen the stem bolt with an Allen key. If you can't pull the stem out, it may be slightly rusted. Give the bolt a few good taps with a rubber mallet; the expander wedge will usually unseat itself easily from the bottom of the stem. Then hold the lower hexagonal nut on the headset in place and unscrew the locknut. You can now remove both nuts and get at the top bearing set. If you pull the forks right out of the frame, you will be able to get at the bottom bearing set, which is located between the fork crown and the head tube.

Clean all parts with benzine or solvent from the bike shop; then inspect the ball bearings. Any damaged ones will have to be replaced; in this case, it usually makes sense to buy a new headset. If everything is in order, pack the bearings in grease and reassemble the headset.

Other systems

Since the large headset spanners are very unwieldy and cannot easily be fitted into a trail tour kit, designers have come up with different ways of fixing the headset in place. With these systems, both nuts can be turned by hand, and the locknut is tightened with Allen key screws let into the sides. So all you need is an Allen key, which should always be part of any trail tool kit. The principle of adjustment is exactly the same as for any standard headset, but the operation can be carried out virtually without tools.

The Aheadset system

The Aheadset system, so called because it is claimed to be superior to ("ahead of") the conventional headset system, is an attempt to redesign this crucial bearing.

Both systems have their advantages and disadvantages of course. The major advantage of the Aheadset is that it is held in place and adjusted solely by means of Allen keys, which makes those unwieldy headset spanners redundant, even for taking the whole thing apart.

In place of the large hexagonal nuts, a new Aheadset-style stem is used to secure the forks. The steerer tube inserts into the stem and is held in place by one or two Allen key bolts in the side of the stem. An Allen key bolt passes through a cap on the top of the stem and threads into a small expanding washer in the steerer. It is this bolt that is used to adjust the headset. As a result, the steerer tube does not have to be threaded; this eliminates the need to reform the thread after the steerer tube has been cut to size prior to fitting a new fork. The disadvantage of the system is that the stem can no longer be adjusted for height except by inserting spacers.

The principle for adjusting the Aheadset system is exactly the same as for a conventional one: there should be just enough play for the headset to turn smoothly without there being any detectable wobble at the handlebars when the front brake is engaged and the bicycle pushed back and forth.

In order to adjust the Aheadset, first loosen the stem clamp bolt/s and then turn the adjuster bolt in a clockwise direction. This will secure the headset and any unwanted slack in the system will disappear.

Check for adjustment in the same way as with a conventional headset: lift the bike up and align the front wheel with the frame. If all is well, the headset will turn smoothly, with no tight spots or play.

The Aheadset consists of the cap through which the adjuster bolt runs, the expanding washer, the clamp ring, the upper bearing races with ball bearings and the lower bearing races with ball bearings (above from left to right).

Disassembling an Aheadset

The procedure for disassembling an Aheadset is even simpler. First unscrew the stem clamp bolt/s and then remove the adjuster bolt and cap. Finally, remove the stem. Now you can simply pull the fork out of the frame from below and dismantle and clean all the individual parts of the headset.

Be careful when cleaning the bike with a high-pressure jet-spray hose. The seal on a headset is often just a rubber ring, and sometimes even this is lacking. If you clean your bike with a jet-spray hose and aim the spray at short range straight at the headset from below, then water may penetrate the bearings and wash out the grease. For this reason, you should always use a jet-spray hose at some distance from a bearing and never aim it directly at such a sensitive component.

The two different types of stem: the Aheadset stem on the left slides over the steerer tube and is held in place by two bolts on the side. The conventional stem on the right fits into the steerer and is held in place by an expander wedge.

Hubs

The hubs on your mountain bike perform their task silently and unobtrusively. Or so we hope, for if they start to draw attention to themselves then it's probably too late. Noises such as grinding or rattling are critical alarm signals.

Modern cycle hubs, like those fitted nowadays to mountain bikes, should last more or less indefinitely. If well-maintained and regularly serviced, the bearings on wheel axles should survive as long as the bike itself. Because of the greater impact loads generated by offroad riding, the hubs fitted to modern mountain bikes are more robust and durable than earlier designs. A ring or labyrinth seal keeps dust, dirt and damp away

from the hub's sensitive inner mechanism. Some manufacturers use a combination of these two types of seal in order to deny access to even the slightest speck of dirt.

However, the best protection for all moving parts in the hub is still a good packing of grease. Grease repels water and dirt. If too much dirt has accumulated inside the hub, or if the grease has been washed away, the dirt particles can eat away at the bearing surfaces within the hub. In order to prevent this happening, both front and rear hubs should be serviced after they have been subjected to abuse, such as frequent submersions in water or a particularly muddy ride.

The grease-guard system

With grease-guard systems, cleaning and greasing are very simple operations. These systems have greasing nipples fitted to the hubs. Fresh grease can be injected through them into the bearings, so that the old grease, together with any accumulated dirt, is forced out of the hubs. However, such a system is usually found only on very expensive, high-performance bikes.

With all other types of hub, the bearings have to be dismantled, cleaned, packed in fresh grease and then reassembled. To do this you will need two cone spanners (very thin spanners designed to fit between the spanner used on the locknut and the hub itself). The commonest sizes of cone spanner are 13/14 mm and 14/15 mm.

Checking hub adjustment

When removing or fitting hubs, you can take the opportunity to check and/or alter the adjustment. If there is too much play in the bearings, you will be able to move the wheel slightly from side to side. This will cause the hub to go out of alignment, eventually destroying the bearings. If the bearings are too tight, the hub will not spin easily or may stick, as if the bearings were jamming slightly. This puts too much pressure on the bearing races and in the longer term will also destroy the hub.

It is relatively simple to disassemble the front hub. Remove the front wheel from the forks (slacken off the brakes, open the quick-release skewers and if necessary unscrew the adjusting nut a little). Remove the quick-release skewers from the hub. The conical tip of the springs on the quick-release skewers should always face inwards, i.e. towards the middle of the hub.

Depending on the model, you will now see the axle protruding on either side of the hub, with a locknut, cone and various spacers and seals on both sides. Quick-release hubs always have hollow axles in order to accommodate the quick-release skewers. These hubs gain their

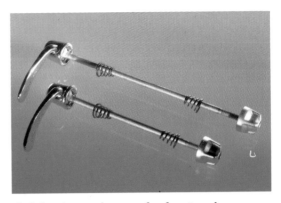

Quick-release skewers for front and rear hubs. The tips of the cone-shaped springs should always point towards the middle of the axle.

stability from the tension generated by the quick-release skewers when they are tightened. The axles used on the most recent designs of mountain bike are larger in diameter. This makes the forks more stable, which is a definite advantage, particularly with modern suspension forks. Suspension forks are more easily distorted than rigid forks because they twist more readily.

Dismantling a hub

Hold the cone (the nut nearest to the hub) in place with a cone spanner and loosen the locknut with a second cone spanner or any other suitable spanner. If you completely unscrew the locknut by hand, you will then get to one or more seals and one or more spacers.

Make a note of the exact sequence and arrangement of these seals and spacers. Write the configuration down, or make yourself a little sketch of the construction of the hub. This will make the task of reassembly considerably easier, and you will avoid unnecessary mistakes. Once you have removed the cone and locknut from one side, together with all the seals and spacers, you can push the axle out of the other side of the hub. It is a good idea to keep the wheel vertical as you do so, otherwise the ball bearings on one side will fall out.

First check the adjustment. If readjustment does not help, the hubs will have to be dismantled. In order to disassemble the axles, first remove the quick-release skewers. Have a number of small tins ready to put the various parts in.

Using cone spanners of the correct size, hold the inner cone in place (bottom spanner) and unscrew the locknut. Make a note of the positions of the spacers and seals.

Once you have unscrewed the cones, the ball bearings in their cups will be revealed. Take care at this point not to lose any of the small silvery balls. The simplest thing to do is to remove the bearings individually with a pair of tweezers. Before you start your work, equip yourself with small tins or lids in which to keep the tiny parts safe.

Paraffin or benzine used to be used to degrease and clean metal parts. Special liquid cleansers are now available in bike shops, some of which contain citric acid or are biodegradable and less damaging to the environment. Paraffin or benzine both have the disadvantage of being highly flammable and strong smelling.

The most effective method of cleaning is to soak all the parts for several hours in cleanser. This allows the cleanser to work properly and dissolve all the old grease and dirt.

Dry and clean all individual components with a cloth. You can now carefully check all bearing surfaces for signs of damage; scratches on the inside surfaces of the hub or on the ball bearings are indications of friction caused by dirt or faulty adjustment. If the bearings are already scored, they should be replaced. In this case, it is best to replace the bearings on both sides. This is certainly cheaper than replacing a complete hub.

If the hub is faulty, the whole wheel will have to be rebuilt. It is much more sensible, far less inconvenient and much cheaper to maintain the hubs properly.

After cleaning, all parts should be greased. Special products for this are available from bike shops. The price of a tube or small tin might seem excessive to some. But remember you only need a few grams, and you might be saving yourself much higher repair costs. The grease has to lubricate, i.e. reduce friction on the bearings and bearing surfaces, but at the same time has to adhere to the moving parts and not be displaced by water. White grease has the advantage of making any contamination by dirt immediately visible when the hub is dismantled. Pack the bearings with plenty of grease.

Reassembling a hub

Now reassemble the parts in reverse sequence. First tighten the cone gently with the cone spanner, then replace the locknut, tightening it gently with the spanner. Now take the axle between your fingers and push it back and forth. It should move only very slightly from side to side. Then spin the axle backwards and forwards with your fingers in order to check whether it is running freely, with no tight spots.

If there is too much lateral play on the axle, you will have to tighten the cone nut a little. If the axle is not running freely or is sticking, you will have to slacken off the cone nut a little (turn it anti-clockwise). If the hub is correctly adjusted as described, hold the cone in place with the cone spanner and tighten up the locknut. Make sure that the cone spanner does not move, otherwise the adjustment of the hub will be altered again.

The same principle applies when it comes to disassembling the rear hub. However, there are more spacers and seals than on the front hub, so you have to pay even greater attention to the order in which the parts are assembled. Once the hubs are fully reassembled, insert the quick-release skewers and put the wheels back in the dropouts. Just one more tip to finish with: don't tighten the cones too tightly, because the design of the quick-release skewers subjects the bearings to additional pressure in any case.

If you twist the outer sealing ring at the hole marked "open", the hub can be greased to a limited extent from the outside. The axle needs to be removed for a more thorough job. Keep the wheel vertical as you remove the axle so that the exposed bearings do not fall out.

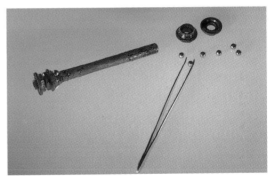

A pair of tweezers is the best tool for removing ball bearings from a hub. Clean the axle and regrease it. Inspect the bearings for damage or signs of wear and replace them if necessary.

The bottom bracket

This bearing takes more punishment than any other on the bike: dirt and stresses pound it from all sides. Once it begins to creak and grind, it's probably too late: one of the ball bearings has split into several parts or so much dirt has penetrated the bearing that it has begun to grind itself to pieces.

Water can penetrate through all possible openings in the frame of a mountain bike (underside of the head tube, seat tube) and accumulate at the lowest point of the frame, near the bottom bracket. Conventional bottom brackets have only a plastic sleeve around the crank, into which moisture can penetrate very easily. If rust begins to eat away at the bottom bracket, it's only a matter of time before it stops working properly or even seizes up altogether. So take good care of the bottom bracket: it is at the heart of the transmission system. If you get the impression when pedalling that the cranks are loose, or they are running out of true, or if there are irritating creaking noises coming from the bottom bracket, it's time to check the bearings.

Maintenance-free cartridge bottom brackets

The simplest types of bottom bracket to maintain and service are fully sealed cartridge bottom brackets and the grease-guard system. The former need absolutely no servicing at all. In fact you couldn't service them even if you wanted to, since they run in a completely sealed shell and are adjusted and lubricated in the factory. Sales of this type have been increasing since 1993. If the sealed unit fails, it has to be replaced as repairs would be so expensive that they are not worthwhile. Special spanners are needed to remove this sort of bracket, although they are not actually very expensive. Anyone who wants to re-equip his or her bike or who is constantly having problems with their bottom bracket because of their weight or their style of riding should buy a fully-sealed cartridge bottom bracket; various sizes are available to fit most frames and chainsets.

The grease-guard system also makes maintenance easy; it is actually only a copy of old bottom bracket designs, reintroduced by resourceful Americans. This type of bottom bracket is equipped with a grease nipple through which fresh grease can be pumped by means of a grease gun. At the same time, the old grease is squeezed out of the bearing, together with any accumulated dirt and water. As soon as the fresh grease starts to spill out, you can be sure that the accumulated dirt has been removed and the bottom bracket axle is clean and running smoothly again.

Checking the bottom bracket

With the type of bottom bracket commonly fitted to mountain bikes – the so-called BSA type – it is possible to adjust the play oneself. A loose bottom bracket usually makes a grinding or creaking noise; sometimes the cranks turn jerkily. The simplest way of checking the bottom bracket is to take the chain off the chainring and turn the cranks. If they turn jerkily or start to stick, there are foreign bodies in the bearing, or it is too tight.

In order to get access to the bottom bracket, remove the cranks. Start by unscrewing the crank bolts with a suitable spanner or Allen key.

A crank extractor should be used in order to remove the cranks from the axle. Lightly grease the crank thread beforehand.

A lockring spanner and a peg spanner are needed to adjust a BSA bottom bracket. To dismantle it, unscrew the lockring on the left-hand side and then unscrew the left-hand bearing cup. For safety reasons, the bottom bracket should be cleaned and regreased once or twice a year.

Check the bottom bracket for excess play by pushing a crank back and forth. If the crank moves to and fro in the direction of the bottom bracket axle, then there is too much play in the bearing and it will have to be adjusted. A grinding noise may be coming from either the cranks or the pedals. Tighten the Allen key bolts on the chainrings, and in particular tighten the crank bolts very firmly, since they often creak or grind even if they are only slightly loose. This procedure should be repeated frequently, since it may take several trips for the crank arms to become firmly seated on the axle. So take this piece of advice seriously, otherwise you may find yourself dismantling the bottom bracket unnecessarily in order to cure the grinding or creaking.

Before starting to adjust or remove the bottom bracket, you must equip yourself with the special tools required, namely a crank extractor and the correct bottom bracket spanners. Using a pipe

wrench will only damage the frame or the bearing cups and may even ruin the whole bike.

Disassembling the bottom bracket

Use the crank extractor to remove the right-hand crank. To do this, first unscrew the crank bolt anti-clockwise and then screw the crank extractor into the recess of the crank arm in order to pull it off the bottom bracket axle. This will expose the left-hand bearing cup, which can be unscrewed with the appropriate spanner. This adjustable cup has holes in it into which a peg spanner (a special spanner with two pegs) can be fitted. In order to disassemble the bottom bracket, the cranks and chainrings have to be removed as well. Then unscrew the locknut on

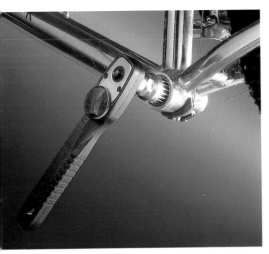

Special spanners, which vary from model to model, are needed to remove modern fully-sealed cartridge bottom brackets.

the left-hand side and unscrew the bearing cup from the frame with the peg spanner. The bottom bracket axle and both bearing cups can then be removed, cleaned and regreased.

It is essential to replace any damaged or scratched parts or bearings.

If you simply want to adjust the bearing, it is sufficient just to remove the left-hand crank arm. This will expose the left-hand side of the bottom bracket and give an unrestricted view of the axle. Then loosen the locknut with a lockring spanner and gently tighten the bearing cup with a peg spanner (turn it clockwise). Check the play by trying to push the bottom bracket axle to and fro. If the axle will hardly move at all from side to side but still turns easily, fasten the bearing cup with the peg spanner and tighten up the lock-

nut. Then, for safety reasons, check again for play and smooth running, replace the crank arm and tighten up the crank bolt.

It usually takes several days for the cranks to settle snugly again on the axle. They usually start to creak after a few hours, making it necessary to tighten them up again. After the third ride at the latest, however, everything should be running smoothly again.

In order to cut down the size and weight of your trail tool kit, it is best to fit the crank arms with Allen key bolts rather than hexagonal nuts and bolts. They can be obtained from specialist shops. Such bolts are a standard fitting on some bikes.

Cartridge bottom brackets are maintenance-free, since they are fully sealed and adjusted by the manufacturer. Should you wish to fit a unit of this kind, check that the axle width is suitable for your bike and that your cranks will fit.

Pedals

The pedals have to support the rider's weight and are constantly exposed to a great deal of stress. And since they are positioned close to the ground, large amounts of dirt also accumulate on them. Modern mountain bike pedals are well sealed, so that under normal circumstances hardly any moisture can penetrate the bearings. The same applies to pedals as to bottom brackets or hubs: if you clean your bike with a jet-spray hose, do so from a safe distance. If you get too close with the hose, the high pressure will displace the seals and water will get into the bearings. In the long term, this will cause the bearings to fail.

Occasionally on cross-country rides, the pedals will bump against a stone or a tree root. Inspect them from time to time to ensure they are still turning smoothly and the axles are not bent. You will usually notice when pedalling whether any part of a pedal is loose or twisted. The warning signal is a grinding or clicking noise, particularly when cycling uphill or standing up to pedal.

Clipless pedals

Step-in or clipless pedals (called SPDs, short for Shimano Pedalling Dynamics), similar to those used by racing cyclists, are becoming increasingly popular with sporty riders. They are a sort of safety pedal that work in conjunction with the appropriate cleats; the rider's feet are held in place by a gripping mechanism similar to that on ski bindings. The rider releases his or her feet by twisting them sideways. Novices may find the firm grip of these pedals somewhat dangerous; sporty mountain bike riders and professionals, however, are firmly convinced of the benefits they offer.

Because the rider's shoes are firmly attached to the pedals, it is impossible to slide off, even on bumpy ground. "Bunny hops" are much easier to perform with clipless pedals. Stiffer soles and the firm grip of the feet on the pedals improve pedalling efficiency. Clipless pedals also make it easier to adopt a technique long known to advanced cyclists, including professional racing cyclists. This involves not only pushing down with the front foot, but also at the same time pulling the crank arm up with the rear-most foot. This makes pedalling much smoother, with the pressure being applied steadily and evenly, and makes it easier to pedal through the dead spots at the top and bottom of each revolution (i.e. the point at which the crank arms are vertical). This technique can be practised but is possible only with toeclips and tightly set straps.

The easiest way to disassemble pedals, whether conventional or clipless, is with a long-handled 15 mm spanner. Hint: to unscrew a pedal, always turn the spanner against the direction of travel.

Pedals need to be serviced only once or twice a year, since they are normally well-sealed. The bearings sit at the end of the axle inside the pedal. A special spanner, supplied with the pedals, is required to remove clipless pedals prior to dismantling the axle.

Toeclips and straps

However, tight straps are dangerous on mountain bikes, because it is difficult for a rider to get his or her feet out of the pedals and on to the ground in dicey situations. Novices should begin riding with just toeclips, without any toestraps. You will then be able to take your foot off the pedal in all directions. The plastic toeclip will stop your foot sliding off the front of the pedal, which can cause painful injuries to the calves and shins. When you come to attach the toestrap, twist it as you pass it through the cage; this will stop it sliding and the buckle will stay in the same place.

Pedals are always screwed into the cranks with a 15 mm spanner. Apply a little grease or solvent to the pedal axle thread, so that it does not get jammed. Take care not to confuse the right-hand and left-hand pedals. The right-side pedal has a right-hand thread and the left-side pedal has a left-hand thread. This means that the left-side pedal has to be screwed in anti-clockwise.

Fitting pedals

Both pedals are screwed in in the same direction. If you are fitting a pedal to a crank arm, turn the spanner in the direction of travel, irrespective of which side of the bike you are working on. This arrangement means that if the pedals do become a little loose, they will tighten up automatically as you pedal. Don't screw the pedals in too tightly, otherwise you will not be able to remove them later. There is a simple and convenient way of screwing the pedals in: if you have loosened them, just hold the pedal axle firmly in place and spin the cranks backwards. The pedals will screw themselves into the crank arms. Most pedals have Allen key holes in the end of the axle which is behind the crank. When out on a ride, therefore, you could if necessary tighten a pedal with an Allen key. If you need to remove a pedal and do not have a long-handled 15 mm spanner, you can use a spanner and an Allen key together at the crank end of the axle in order to exert greater leverage. If you frequently remove the pedals from your bike (in order to transport it for example) and the thread is kept well greased, you should be able to manage with a multi-tool that has an Allen key or with a long Allen key.

Dismantling pedals

If the pedal is sticking or making loud clicking noises, the axle will have to be dismantled. For this you will need a cone spanner of the appropriate size. A special tool is required for clipless pedals, which is normally supplied with the pedals. By unscrewing the cone between the thread and the body of the pedal, the axle can be removed and inspected. The ball bearings are located at the end of the axle; they must always be well greased.

The special tool used for clipless pedals has the direction of turn marked on it (clockwise for the right pedal, anti-clockwise for the left pedal). The tool is a plastic attachment that fits into the gaps on the axle nut. The plastic collar is shifted with a 36 mm combination spanner, like the one used to adjust the headset. However, a large number of turns is required before the axle can be removed from the pedal body, so don't let yourself get irritated.

The release tension on clipless pedals is adjusted by means of a bolt. This tension adjuster bolt can be screwed inwards (clockwise) with an Allen key to increase the tension: this will make it more difficult to release your feet. If the bolt is turned anti-clockwise, the tension will be backed off

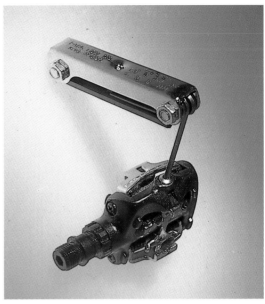

The release tension of clipless pedals can be adjusted by means of an Allen key. Turning the screw inwards will increase tension, and vice versa. Do not go beyond the maximum markings for the adjuster screws.

and it will be easier to release your feet from the pedals. The pedals have minimum and maximum markings on them which should not be exceeded; otherwise the spring-loaded adjusting bolts will drop out of the pedal.

Clean clipless pedals regularly in order to get rid of all the accumulated dirt and grit, and pack the springs with plenty of grease; otherwise the tension in the release mechanism may increase, or the pedal may even lock altogether – and that can be painful.

Gears

The early mountain bikes had only five gears; the norm nowadays is 21 or 24. However, not all 21 gears are actually available for use. In reality, there are only about 14 "real" gears to choose from. Some gears overlap with others that offer virtually identical ratios. The theoretical maximum number of 21 is obtained purely arithmetically by multiplying the number of front chainrings (3) by the number of rear sprockets (7).

This type of gear mechanism, brought to a state of virtual perfection by Japanese manufacturers, is intended to offer as wide a range of gear ratios as possible. The ratio is determined by the relative sizes of the chainring at the front and the sprocket at the rear. With a 52-tooth chainring, a complete turn of the cranks will turn a rear sprocket with 26 teeth twice, producing a gear ratio of 2:1.

The gear systems on mountain bikes offer a very wide range of ratios, ranging from a very low ratio of 0.75:1 (24–32), suitable for hill climbing, to a very high ratio of 4:1 (48–12), which is very hard to push. The front mechanism or derailleur is controlled by the lever or shifter on the left-hand grip. The rear mechanism or derailleur is controlled by the shifter on the right-hand grip.

Whether you opt for over-handlebar, under-handlebar or twist-grip shifters is purely a matter of personal preference. All three systems have advantages and disadvantages, which you can only discover for yourself through extensive test runs.

The gear-shifting mechanism works in exactly the same way whatever type of shifter is attached to the handlebars. A cable moves the front derailleur (mounted above the chainrings) or the rear derailleur (fitted in the rear dropout) to the left or the right, thus shifting the chain from one chainring or sprocket to another. With modern indexed gears, each gear has its own slot and the chain always moves exactly one sprocket up or down (provided everything's adjusted properly). To be more precise, the chain actually moves just beyond the sprocket and then falls back on to it. Travel-adjusting screws built into the derailleur mechanisms prevent the chain from jumping off the inner and outermost cogs. In order to make gear adjustment easier for you, the commonest problems are described below, together with tips on how to deal with them.

Front derailleur

The chain moves slowly or only with difficulty from the small to the middle or large chainring, it rubs against the front mechanism or jumps over the middle chainring when changing down:
Check the play on the cable that operates the front mechanism. To do this, shift the chain on to the smallest chainring: the cable should now be slack, but not excessively so. If the cable can be lifted up by more than two or three millimetres (⅛ to ³⁄₁₆ in), it needs tightening. This can be done with the barrel adjuster on the shifter. Unscrew the barrel adjuster in half-turns (anti-clockwise) until the slack in the cable is taken up but the front mechanism remains at rest. If the degree of adjustment available through the barrel adjuster is not sufficient, the cable will have to be adjusted at the front mechanism by releasing the Allen key screw and gently pulling the cable through with a pair of pliers.

The chain cannot be shifted at all, or only with difficulty, on to the largest chainring:
Unscrew the outer travel-adjusting screw on the front derailleur by half a turn (anti-clockwise). If the mechanism is still not working properly, unscrew it another half-turn, until the chain drops on to the largest chainring. If the outer derailleur cage plate is still rubbing against the chain, unscrew the same screw a further quarter of a turn.

The chain keeps coming off the inner chainring:
Tighten up the inner travel-adjusting screw on the front derailleur by half a turn (in a clockwise direction). If it is still not working properly, tighten it a further half a turn, until the chain no longer falls off the smallest chainring.

The chain keeps coming off the outer chainring:
Tighten the outer travel-adjusting screw by half a turn (in a clockwise direction). If this doesn't work, tighten it a further half-turn, until the chain no longer slips off the largest chainring.

The chain will not drop on to the smallest chainring:
Unscrew the inner travel-adjusting screw by half a turn. If the chain will still not drop on to the smallest chainring, unscrew the adjusting mechanism a further half-turn. If the inner cage plate is still rubbing against the chain, repeat the procedure, but this time in quarter-turns.

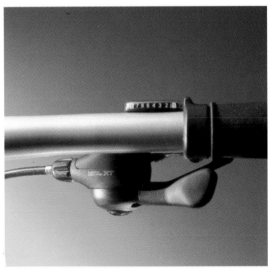

An unassuming but important part of the gear shifting mechanism: the barrel adjuster on the shifters controls the function of the indexed gears. By unscrewing it you increase the cable tension, and vice versa. Make sure you adjust it by quarter- and half-turns only.

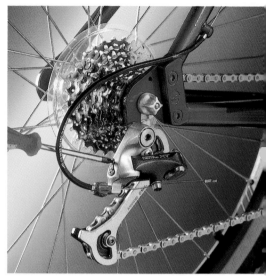

The rear derailleur has two travel-adjusting screws just like the front mechanism. If the chain gets caught between the smallest sprocket and the rear dropout, tighten this screw. If the chain will not shift to the smallest sprocket, slacken the screw off a little.

If the chain drops off the largest chainring, tighten this screw. If the chain will not climb up to the largest chainring even though the cable tension is correctly adjusted, slacken the screw off a little.

If the front derailleur is still not functioning properly despite these adjustments, shift the chain on to the largest chainring and check the position of the mechanism. The outer cage plate should sit exactly parallel to the largest chainring (when viewed from above) and two to three millimetres (about 1/8 to 3/16 in) above the teeth on the chainring (viewed from the side). If this is not the case, loosen the front derailleur mounting clamp on the seat tube with an Allen key and position the mechanism as described above. Then readjust the shifter cable.

The lower travel-adjusting screw on the rear derailleur controls the movement of the chain up to the largest sprocket. If the chain falls between this sprocket and the spokes, tighten this screw. If the chain will not climb up to the largest sprocket, loosen the screw a little.

This is what the front derailleur looks like when adjusted for optimum performance, with a three millimetre gap between the large chainring and the cage. Looked at from above, the front derailleur must be exactly parallel to the outer chainring.

The tension screw on the rear derailleur: if the chain rattles, the cage is too close to the sprockets and the screw should be tightened.

If the chain keeps dropping off the smallest chainring, tighten up the inner travel-adjusting screw on the front derailleur.

The gear cable must be arranged neatly in an arc, without kinks. The rear barrel adjuster, like those on the shifters at the front, can also be used to alter cable tension. Again, proceed by quarter- and half-turns only.

Rear derailleur

Chain shifting is taking too long, the chain is rubbing on the sprockets:
As with the front derailleur, the shifter cable is too slack. In this instance, there are two barrel adjusters that can be used to correct the fault, one on the shifter and one on the rear mechanism itself. Turn one of the adjusters anti-clockwise in half-turn stages until the fault is eliminated.

The chain gets jammed between the largest sprocket and the spokes (see picture p. 44):
Tighten the lower travel-adjusting screw on the rear of the mechanism half a turn. If this produces no improvement, tighten it a further half-turn until the chain no longer drops off the largest sprocket. Viewed from the rear, the upper guide pulley should be sitting directly under the innermost sprocket.

The chain drops between the smallest sprocket and the frame:
Tighten the upper travel-adjusting screw on the rear of the mechanism half a turn. If this does not correct the fault, tighten it a further half-turn until the chain no longer drops off the smallest sprocket. Viewed from the rear, the upper guide pulley should be sitting directly below the outer sprocket (see picture p. 44).

The chain will not shift at all, or only with difficulty, on to the largest sprocket:
Loosen the lower travel-adjusting screw half a turn. If this produces no improvement, loosen it another half-turn until the chain climbs up to the largest sprocket.

The chain will not shift at all, or only with difficulty, on to the smallest sprocket:
Loosen the upper travel-adjusting screw on the rear of the mechanism half a turn. If that doesn't work, loosen it a further half-turn,

Special tools for modern sprocket clusters: the chain whip holds the sprockets in place while the freewheel remover is used to unscrew the sprockets from the axle.

until the chain shifts on to the smallest sprocket.

The chain rattles on the smallest sprocket, and catches when you pedal backwards:
The cage is too close to the sprockets. Tighten the tension screw (clockwise), which is located on the mechanism close to the dropout. At the same time, spin the cranks backwards. If the chain runs backwards without catching, the tension screw is correctly adjusted (see picture p. 45).

When changing down, the chain rubs or will not shift quickly and precisely:
The cables are dirty and there is too much friction between the inner and outer cables. Remove the cables, clean the inners and coat them with a lubricant such as Teflon (oil is too sticky and attracts dirt). Replace the cables at least once and preferably twice a year. Indexed gear systems rely very heavily on properly functioning cables for efficient operation.

If these measures do not help, then the chain or the sprockets are too worn and will have to be replaced.

Keeping your hands clean:
If the chain falls between the smallest chainring and the frame, there is no need to take hold of it. Shift into middle gear and keep pedalling carefully. The front derailleur will lift the chain back on to the chainring. This trick works just as well in the reverse direction, when the chain has fallen to the right off the largest chainring. Shift into middle gear and continue to pedal carefully.

If you want to change the gear ratios or need to fit a new sprocket cluster, you will need the correct freewheel remover and a chain whip. The chain whip is used to hold the sprocket in place, thus preventing the freewheel from turning it, while the freewheel tool is used to unscrew the lockring on the sprocket cluster in an anti-clockwise direction.

Chains

Even the strongest mountain bike is only as good as the weakest link in its chain. Regular inspection and a drop of oil from time to time will extend its working life.

A chain has more than 400 individual parts working together constantly just to make sure you keep rolling forwards as you pedal. Each link in a bicycle chain consists of pins, links and rollers, which may come apart from time to time. Gear systems now make much greater demands of chains than they used to: they have to jump from one sprocket to another in the space of only two revolutions of the cog, and have to deflect a long way in order to do so.

Despite all attempts to find an alternative means of transmitting power from the cranks to the rear wheel, chains have remained in use up to the present day. All other systems, such as the cardan drive or belt drive systems, are either much heavier or else less efficient. A roller chain system is one of the most efficient methods of transmitting power: only approximately 2 per cent of the power input is lost on the way to the rear wheel.

The chain tool

Modern bike chains are much more flexible than their predecessors; because of this, they no longer have a master link that can be opened or closed with a pair of pliers or a screwdriver. Chains for six- to eight-speed freewheels are narrow, endless chains. Breaking and joining a chain is possible only with a chain tool, also known as a chain splitter. Chain tools are available in two sizes: one for the workshop and a more compact version for the trail tool kit.

Always take a chain tool with you. If the chain breaks on you, there is no way of putting it back together again. If you are lucky and the pin has not completely fallen out of the link, you may be able to drive it back in with a chain tool, or by knocking it in carefully with a stone.

The right time to change the chain

Even a modern bicycle chain will not last for ever. It should be replaced at least every 3,500 km (2,000 miles or so), if not more frequently. Because of the grime, mud and damp to which it is exposed on cross-country rides, the chain on a mountain bike wears more quickly than that on a road bike, and more frequent gear changes subject it to greater stresses. A worn chain will also damage the sprockets and the chainrings, causing more wear and tear and impairing gear shifting. So the chain should be examined from time to time and given a few drops of lubricant. It should never be allowed to dry out.

If you service and lubricate your bicycle regularly, you will be able to use synthetic lubricants on the chain and the guide pulleys. These lubricants form a water-repellent film, and any irritating squeaking noises usually disappear immediately. However, the lubricating effect does not last long. Specialist chain oils, available from bike shops, offer longer-lasting protection, but their stickiness attracts more dirt and grime, making it necessary to clean the chain thoroughly from time to time. Special chain cleaners are available

for this purpose; they consist of a small plastic box with built-in brushes into which cleaning solvent is poured. Or you can dismantle the chain and soak it for a few hours in cleaning solvent before relubricating it.

Testing for wear

There is an easy way to find out whether or not a bicycle chain is worn: simply lift it up with your hands or a screwdriver as far as possible from one of the front chainrings. If you can lift it more than 3 millimetres (about 1/8 to 3/16 in) from the chainwheel teeth it will have to be replaced.

If the chain jumps – which can cause some unpleasant surprises, particularly when standing up to climb extremely steep sections – the usual cause is one or two stiff links. This stiffness may be the result of "chain suck", when the chain drops off the smallest chainring and ends up jammed between the frame and the crank or chainring. But it can also occur after a repair. Look for the stiff spot and free it up by waggling the offending links to and fro between your fingers.

In order to break a modern bicycle chain, a chain tool must be used to remove a pin. Positioning the tool on the outside and on the bottom of the chain will give the greatest room for manoeuvre. Take care not to bend the pin.

Take care not to push the pin completely out of the link plate. Otherwise you will have to sac-rifice two links in order to join the chain up again.

Splitting a chain

You must proceed very carefully when splitting a chain with a chain tool. Under no circumstances must you push the pin all the way out, other-wise you will be unable to drive it back in again. At your workbench at home, you might just be able to do so with pliers and a vice, but the chances of success out in the rain or in fading light are virtually nil, and you will have to sacrifice two links in order to join the chain up again.

The best thing to do when splitting a chain is to leave the pin protruding just half a millimetre on the inside of the link plate. This makes it easier to snap in the next link and to use the chain tool

to drive the pin back in. New chains for the HyperGlide system are rejoined by a special pin that is twice as long as a normal pin. This stronger pin is driven back in with a HyperGlide chain tool; finally, the excess is broken off with pliers at the break point engraved on the pin. This means that the very flexible HyperGlide chain is more securely joined than with a normal pin.

Make sure the chain is fitted correctly before dri-ving in the final pin. Thread it through the front mechanism first, around the rear sprocket and then round the front of the guide pulley at the top of the rear mechanism and round the back of the tension pulley at the bottom before joining it up at the front chainring again.

Testing for wear: if the chain can be lifted more than three millimetres ($^3/_{16}$ in) from the chain-rings, it should be replaced.

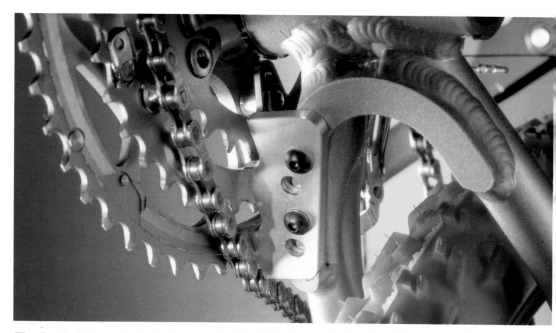

The "anti-chain suck device" prevents the chain becoming jammed between the chainrings and the frame.

Place the chain on the smallest of the front chainrings when fitting it; this will place less strain on the chain. When replacing the last pin, always position the chain tool on the outside and at the lowest point of the chain's path, where you have the greatest room for manoeuvre.

Correcting the chain length

The correct length for the chain depends on the type of bike and gear system. Shift the chain on to the largest chainring at the front and the smallest sprocket at the rear. The rear cage should now be absolutely vertical, and the two pulleys should be exactly in line with each other. As the chain wears, it stretches and it eventually becomes necessary to shorten it by removing a link.

If you fit a new sprocket cluster, you should also renew the chain at the same time, since an old chain would cause excessive wear on the new cogs.

This chain has a stiff link after being dismantled. In order to free up the link, waggle it to and fro between your fingers.

Wheels

Despite all the high-tech developments on mountain bikes, the wheels are still designed in pretty much the same way as those on the very earliest bicycles. There are, it is true, futuristic designs made of carbon and ceramics, but they have not yet gained widespread acceptance. There is a good reason for this: a spoked wheel is easier to repair when out on a ride.

A bicycle wheel functions like a good crime novel: it depends on tension. The rims on mountain bike wheels have become increasingly more robust, but it is the spokes that are decisive in determining whether a wheel runs true. They must all be under the correct tension so that the wheel runs smoothly without any lateral or vertical misalignment.

Mountain bike wheels are subjected to extreme stresses: they tear over tree roots and stones, branches sometimes get jammed in the spokes and sporty riders make jumps of several yards, bringing the wheels crashing down and subjecting them to even greater strain. Even the thickest spokes may fail in the face of such abuse. And yet a buckled wheel is not such a big deal. With just a simple spoke key, a bent wheel can be brought back into shape, even out in the open country. If the rim is completely distorted, an emergency repair will be necessary, with the fine tuning being left until you get home. If the rim is rubbing too much against the brake blocks after the emergency repair, slacken off the brake cable in question and ride home – with care – on just one brake.

Truing a wheel

It is important to equip yourself with a spoke key, which fits over the spoke nipples. If you work a lot on your bike, it might be worth investing in a wheel stand. With one of these, and a great deal of time, skill and intuition, you will be able to restore your rims to their original condition in the peace and quiet of your own home. However, not everyone has the patience for this. There is no mystery about wheel truing, but there are cyclists who swear by a particular mechanic who, they claim, has the gift of truing wheels to perfection.

It is simpler just to use the dropouts to true a wheel, although this makes perfection more difficult to achieve. In this case, use the brake blocks as reference points. Turn the wheel and apply the brakes lightly. The rim will rub at the point of greatest error, and this is where the spoke key will have to be used. The principle is to tighten the spokes on the opposite side of the rim to the misalignment; the spokes in the middle of the wobble should be tightened more than the spokes to the right and left of it. So if the rim wobbles to the right (looking in the direction of travel), tighten the spokes that lead to the rim from the left-hand side of the hub.

The head of the spoke nipple is located on the inside of the rim; the visible part sits like a nut on the spoke thread. Screwing the nipple further on to the spoke shortens the spoke and increases the tension. So to tension a spoke, the spoke key is turned anti-clockwise (as viewed from the centre of the wheel). Conversely, a spoke can be slackened off by turning the nipple key clockwise.

A spoke key is used to adjust the tension in the spokes and thus even out lateral or vertical misalignment. Turning the key anti-clockwise (looking at it from the centre of the wheel) increases tension, and vice versa.

Lateral adjustment

In order to correct lateral bending, tighten the spoke at the point of greatest error by half a turn, then back off the two spokes to the right and left on the same side by a quarter-turn. Repeat this process until the wheel no longer wobbles from side to side.

If the spokes will not take any further tension, do things the other way round. Carefully slacken off the spokes on the side of the wobble. There is an easy way of evening up the tension in the spokes. Tap the spokes with a screwdriver or spanner. Spokes with the same degree of tension will produce the same note when tapped, just like the strings of a musical instrument. Slack spokes will produce deeper notes, and vice versa.

This technique can be used to true a wheel to within a few tenths of a millimetre. In order to get the lateral alignment absolutely perfect, and in particular to correct vertical distortion, you will need a wheel stand, or truing jig. The wheel is clamped inside the stand without the tyre, and there are adjustable reference points parallel to and in front of the rim that help to get the wheel trued perfectly.

Vertical adjustment

With vertical distortion the wheel wobbles up and down, not from side to side. In order to correct this fault, all the spokes adjacent to the point of error have to be tightened, or the spokes on the opposite side have to be slackened. Again,

Correcting lateral misalignment: tighten the spokes opposite the point of greatest error in half-turns. Tighten the spokes to the right and left (marked on the photo) in quarter-turns.

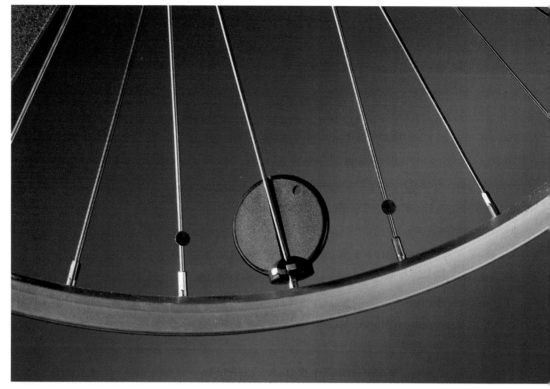

Correcting vertical misalignment: if the rim wobbles up and down, tighten all the spokes at the point of error (marked on the photo) in order to bring the rim back into shape.

you should proceed in small steps, turning the spokes by half- and quarter-turns only.

If you are taking your mountain bike out on a long ride, it is definitely worth taking a few spare spokes of exactly the right size required for your particular bike. It is true that improved materials and special shaping mean that spokes are much less likely to break nowadays, but accidents can still happen. There are even butted and double-butted spokes, which are thicker at one or both ends, and therefore stronger.

Spare spokes can be stored in the seat tube (for example), which should then be sealed with a cork, or they can be taped to the seat stays.

Emergency spokes

If a spoke breaks on the sprocket side of the wheel, you will also need a freewheel remover in order to be able to fit a new spoke. For this kind of emergency, it is possible to buy wire spokes that are attached by a hook rather than a nipple; they can be rolled up for carrying on the bike. These emergency spokes, which should be cut to the right length before you leave home, will be enough to get you home or to the next "refuge" on your planned route.

With the aid of a wheel stand and a certain amount of patience, wheels can be trued to the last millimetre.

Repairing punctures

Even the thickest bicycle tyres sometimes get a flat. All you need to repair a puncture is two tyre levers, a puncture repair kit, a pump and five minutes' time.

Knobbly mountain bike tyres are not immune to punctures. Although they are relatively impervious to fragments of glass or small nails, they are not totally invulnerable. And what's more, mountain bike fanatics are in the habit of riding over hard, stony ground where a conventional bike would make no headway at all.

Impact punctures are another problem that may occur when the bike is ridden at high speeds or over stony ground. They are caused by the edge of the rim pinching the inner tube from inside. The result is a characteristic double hole in the tube. The best protection against these "snakebites", as the Americans call them, is to keep the tyre pressures fairly high. While it is true that pressures lower than 2.1 kg/cm² (30 lb/in²) make for a more comfortable ride, the risk of an impact puncture rises alarmingly. Depending on the weight of the rider, pressures between 2.45 and 3.15 kg/cm² (35 and 45 lb/in²) have proved effective. If you drive a lot on metalled roads, you can of course increase the pressures. Lighter riders who also show greater restraint and caution can reduce the pressure a little.

At home in your workshop, a flat tyre is no problem; out in the open country, it is much more difficult to deal with. And accidents usually happen when you least expect them.

Repair kit and pump

So you should always have a repair kit and a pump with you. A spare inner tube makes repairs easier, but what do you do if you have a second puncture? A tube of good old rubber solution and a few patches take up very little room and don't weigh a lot either. And there are now plenty of lightweight pumps that can be carried securely on the bike. They usually have adaptors to fit the two common valve systems. Expensive CO_2 cartridges, on the other hand, can only be used once. They might be useful under certain circumstances in a race, but not for a cyclist who rides averagely difficult routes and can afford to spend a little time changing a tyre.

The two commonest valve systems are known as Schrader and Presta. The former is a thick valve, like that on a car tyre; the latter is thinner and has a barrel that needs to be loosened before the tyre is inflated.

One of the advantages of Schrader valves is that they can be inflated easily with a garage airline. Inner tubes fitted with a Presta valve are a little lighter and are secured with a lockring.

However, Presta valves are also more delicate and buckle easily if the pump is pressed too hard against them. Yet they are easier to pump up, and because they were developed from road racing, they can be inflated to higher pressures.

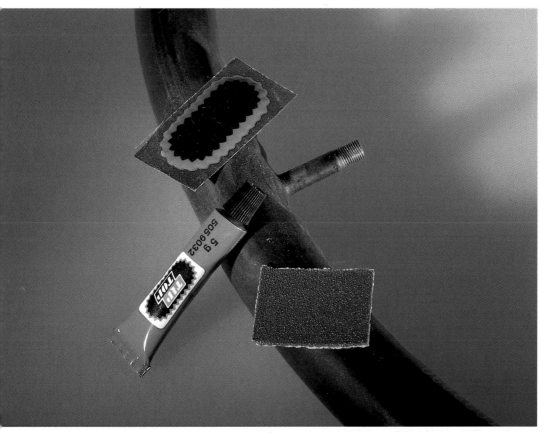

Roughen the area around the puncture and cover it with rubber solution. The sticky area should be larger than the patch you are going to apply. It is essential to leave the rubber solution to dry for five minutes before you press the patch firmly in place.

Tyre levers

Do not forget your tyre levers: a mountain bike tyre is much tougher than a normal one. A couple of plastic tyre levers weigh only a few grams (ounces) and really make tyre changing very much easier. Insert a tyre lever between the rim and the outer tyre casing and then push in the second tyre lever. Hook one of the levers around a spoke (this is why tyre levers have a little notch at one end) and run the second one between the rim and the outer tyre casing in order to unhook the tyre.

You need to take only one side of the tyre off the rim in order to be able to remove the inner tube. Having done that, carefully feel around the inside of the tyre and the rim in order to locate any foreign bodies such as nails or thorns. Even a spoke nipple protruding through the rim can cause a puncture.

Next inflate the inner tube a little in order to find the puncture. Hold the tube to your ear; you should be able to hear and feel the air escaping. If you put the tube in a bowl of water, the escaping air will form bubbles, revealing the precise location of the hole.

The area around the hole should be roughened slightly (if there is no sandpaper in the repair kit, a rough stone will do the job) and covered with a thin, even coating of rubber solution. Make sure you spread the adhesive over an area larger than the patch you are going to apply. Now be patient for five minutes. The rubber solution has to dry, otherwise the patch will not adhere properly to the tube. After the five minutes have elapsed, press the patch firmly over the hole and then flatten it down with a blunt object, such as a screwdriver handle or the edge of a tyre lever. A word of caution: with a "snakebite" impact puncture, there will be two holes side by side, so use a large oval patch, or two small ones.

Any obstinate mountain bike tyre can be unhooked from the rim with the aid of two tyre levers. Insert one lever and then the other between the rim and the outer casing of the tyre. Hook one of the levers over a spoke and then run the second one round the rim in order to unhook the tyre.

There are two different types of valves for mountain bikes. On the left is a Presta valve, on the right a Schrader valve. Good pumps have adaptors for both types of valve.

Push the tube, still partially inflated, back between the tyre and the rim and press the tyre back into place over the wheel rim.

You will find it easier to replace the tyre if you stretch it a little first. To do this, it obviously has to be removed completely from the rim. Place both feet on the tyre and pull it up sharply with both hands. Repeat this procedure all the way round the tyre. It should then slip more easily into place on the rim. You can of course also use the tyre levers to persuade particularly recalcitrant tyres back on to the rim.

Positioning the valve

You must ensure that the valve stem is perfectly upright in the valve hole. If it is not, straighten it and then pump the inner tube up a little more. It is advisable at this point to run your fingers all the way round the rim to make sure that the outer casing is properly in place and that the inner tube is not trapped. Only then should you pump the tyre up fully.

If the puncture has been caused by a brake block slitting open the tyre, jam a piece of paper (e.g. a banknote) or a sliver of bark into the gash so that the inner tube does not bulge out. If you have fitted a spare tube rather than repairing the puncture, just tie a knot in the punctured tube to remind you to repair it on the next wet Sunday afternoon.

And to finish with, here are two more pieces of advice. Firstly, when removing the wheels for repairs, shift the chain on to the smallest rear sprocket (i.e. the highest gear). This will make it easier to get the rear wheel on and off.

Secondly, never use a screwdriver or any other sharp tool, such as a spanner, to unhook the tyre. You will probably damage both the rims and the tube, making it impossible to repair the puncture at all.

Emergency repairs

Most breakdowns and accidents happen when you are not expecting them and are least able to deal with them. Here are a few tips to keep you in the saddle until you get home: you're better off riding a damaged bike than walking home.

In contrast to other forms of cycle racing, the rules of mountain bike racing do not allow riders to carry spare parts or receive help from others. So professional racers have to repair all faults and breakdowns themselves. The same can happen to you during a day's riding. In the event of a breakdown, you will be thrown back on to your own resources.

However, with a basic minimum of equipment, you should be able to deal with virtually any problem that might arise.

Compact, lightweight multi-tools, a puncture repair kit and a pump are absolutely indispensable. These items can be carried with no difficulty at all in a seatpack or a frame bag. You should also equip yourself with the basic emergency tool kit shown in the picture on p. 64 and carry it with you at all times. Particularly cautious riders will add spare parts such as an inner tube, brake and gear cables and emergency spokes. A roll of adhesive tape comes in handy for many emergency repairs.

Broken chain

A chain tool is absolutely essential; without one, it is virtually impossible to repair a chain out in the wilds. Compact versions are available that will fit into a jacket or jersey pocket. If the chain breaks, you will need a lot of luck and a great deal of skill to join it up again without a chain tool. To have any chance of success at all, the pin will have to be still in the link; if it falls out in open country, you will almost certainly be unable to find it. Using the inner link as a guide for the pin, try to knock it back into the outer link with a stone. If you manage this, join the chain up again and hammer the pin right in. However, this method is extremely laborious and is seldom successful.

Things are easier with a chain tool. Simply remove a link from the chain, leaving a pin sticking out of the plate, and then join the chain up again. With a little practice, this procedure will take only a few minutes.

The chain tool is also needed to deal with other emergencies. If a thick branch gets jammed in the spokes of the rear wheel and tears the rear mechanism off, or if the rear mechanism is so bent after a crash that it is no longer functioning, select a gear in which you can cope with most types of terrain (running the chain to the middle sprocket at the rear and the middle chainring at the front, for example) and then shorten the chain so that it exactly fits this combination of cogs. This will reduce your choice of gears to one, but you will at least be able to ride rather than walk home.

Punctures

A puncture repair kit, a pump and tyre levers are another essential part of an emergency tool kit (see p. 60), since punctures are a common enough occurrence on mountain bikes. Even without a repair kit, however, you may still be able to ride on. Find the hole in the tube and tie a very, very tight knot in it at exactly that point. This will plug the leak relatively well. You may have to get off now and again to pump up the tyre, but the tube should be reasonably airtight. Even if you don't have a pump, you don't have to resort to walking home. Gather together some grass, leaves, pieces of soft bark or whatever else you can find and use it to stuff the tyre with. You will then be able to ride home slowly without ruining your rims.

Loose screws and bolts

The best way of dealing with loose screws and bolts is to carry a multi-tool with various Allen keys and screwdrivers on it. Multi-tools with an integral chain tool are also available. The screwdriver blade can also be used to tighten a loose bottom bracket, for example. Place the screwdriver in one of the notches on the lockring and hit it with a stone so that the lockring turns in a clockwise direction.

Most screws and bolts on a bike (saddle, stem, brakes, handlebars, control levers) can be tightened up with just two Allen keys. If you want to play it safe, replace the hexagonal bolts on the cranks with Allen key bolts, for which special conversion kits are available. An Allen key is also needed for Aheadset systems. You can try to fix a loose conventional headset as well as you can with your bare hands. An additional 10 mm spanner will be enough for brake adjustments (see pp. 22ff.). The cables on many cantilever brakes are held in place by hexagonal bolts. Replacing them with Allen key bolts will reduce the number of tools you need to carry.

Gears

To guard against all eventualities, you can take spare inners for gears and brakes with you. An electrical connector can be used to repair a cable in an emergency. If the rear derailleur cable breaks, you can continue with just one gear. Screw in the upper travel-adjusting screw (see pp. 42 ff.) until the chain remains stuck on one of the middle sprockets. You can obtain the same effect by jamming a piece of wood into the gear mechanism, thus preventing it from moving.

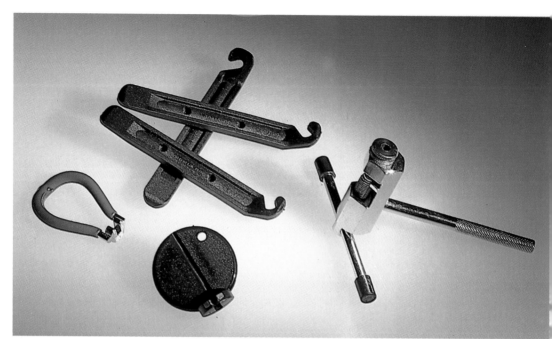

The minimalist tool kit for emergencies: a chain tool is indispensable and spoke keys and tyre levers are useful, as are a spare inner tube or a puncture repair outfit. Tyre levers are light and come in very handy. These tools will fit into a saddlebag.

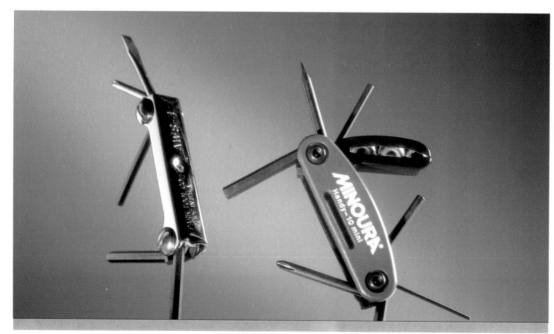

Small and practical: multi-tools have Allen keys of various sizes and usually two screwdriver blades.

If the gear mechanism fails or is torn off, use a chain tool to shorten the chain and turn the bike into a single-speed machine.

Spokes

If a spoke breaks, slacken off the brake cable so that the rim is no longer catching against the brake block. Use a spoke key to true the wheel so that the rim will no longer catch even with the brake back in its operating position. You may need to screw in the barrel adjuster on the brake lever a little in order to move the blocks away from the rim.

Broken parts

Only makeshift repairs are possible if a part breaks during a day's riding. It is a good idea to take a roll of insulating tape or similar adhesive tape with you. You can use it to "splint" a broken handlebar or a snapped seat post.

Your emergency tool kit (see also pp. 15 ff.) is best carried in a small saddlebag, which can be bought in various designs and sizes. If you are in the habit of carrying your bike over rough ground, a triangular bar suspended between the seat and top tubes will also double as a shoulder pad.

Fitting suspension forks

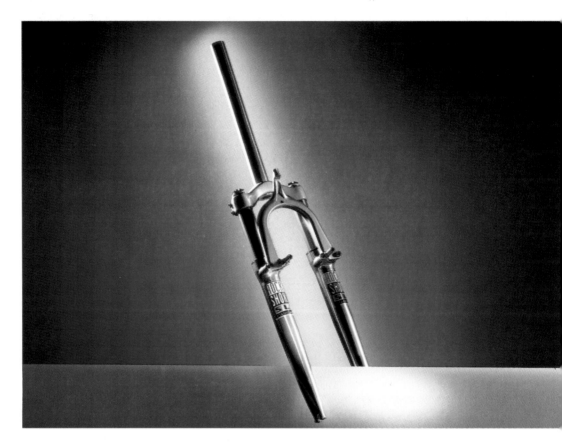

Their introduction was greeted with derision, but they are now state of the art: suspension forks for mountain bikes have become accepted. They provide a comfortable ride and improved safety on downhill stretches.

More and more manufacturers are now offering mountain bikes with factory-fitted suspension forks. However, you don't have to sell your bike and buy a new one, because suspension forks can be fitted as an aftermarket device to your current bike. But you do need some experience in stripping down and reassembling bikes, or an experienced friend you can ask for assistance.

If you don't feel sufficiently confident or experienced, leave the job to a specialist. The forks are an important part of the steering system, and a botched job could be disastrous. Misuse or unauthorised modifications may void the manufacturer's guarantee, so that in the event of damage or injury you will in all probability have to suffer the consequences yourself.

There are two crucial dimensions on your mountain bike when it comes to fitting suspension forks: the diameter and length of the head tube. Equally critical is the headset system.

With conventional headsets, the steerer tube is threaded; with Aheadset systems, this thread is not necessary.

Choosing the right model

Suspension forks for mountain bikes are no longer in their infancy. After several years of development and improvement, they weigh a little over 1 kilogram (2 pounds) and have up to 5 centimetres (2 inches) travel. There are many models on the market that have dampers already fitted by the manufacturer. Two different types of telescopic forks dominate the market: some use elastomer foam rubbers to provide the shock-absorbing medium, others use air spring and oil dampers.

If you decide to fit suspension forks, you should also change over to the new Aheadset system. This will enable you to remove the forks much more quickly and easily with just one Allen key. Suspension forks require regular servicing, and the new headset system simplifies the task.

When buying suspension forks, make sure you obtain the right size, and ask your dealer whether the model you have in mind is suitable for your frame. In the early years of their development, telescopic forks had an adverse effect on the geometry of mountain bikes. Suspension forks altered the head tube angle and affected fork trail, making bikes less manoeuvrable and the handling heavier. Newer designs have solved this problem. Frame builders have also reacted to the boom and now make frames with the appropriate geometry for suspension forks.

The correct diameter

The diameter of the head tube on your bike will affect your choice of fork. Depending on the frame material and the manufacturer, the steerer tube may be 25.4, 28.6 or 31.75 mm (1, 1⅛ or 1¼ in) in diameter. The length of the head tube also varies from frame to frame. Suspension forks are normally supplied with a long steerer tube that is then cut to size with a metal-cutting saw. It's best to take your bike with you when you go to buy your suspension forks.

Begin by removing the handlebars, together with the brake levers and gear shifters. The easiest way of removing the grips is with washing-up liquid or spittle. Lift up the edge of the grip by sticking a small Allen key or screwdriver under it. Then squirt a little washing-up liquid inside, distributing it evenly round the grip. Leave it for a minute or so to take effect; you should then be able to pull the grip off without difficulty.

As for the control levers, loosen the Allen key bolts that attach them to the bars and pull them off. Slackening off the brake cable will give you more room for manoeuvre. You need only take the levers off one side in order to slide the handlebars out of the stem. To do this, unscrew the Allen key clamp bolt that holds the bars in place. If the bars won't move, open up the stem a little by carefully inserting a screwdriver blade.

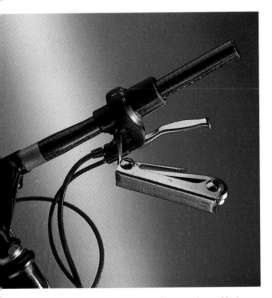

To remove the handlebars, first take off the grips and the control levers by undoing the Allen key bolts underneath the brake lever.

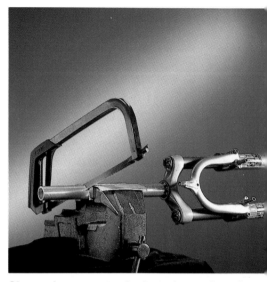

Before dismantling the old forks, remove all components such as the stem and the brake arms. Cantilever brakes can be easily unscrewed with an Allen key. Make sure you reassemble the various parts of the brake arm in the right order.

Clamp the steerer tube in a vice and cut it to the right length with a hacksaw. If you are fitting the same type of headset, just take the length from the old forks. Aheadset systems are supplied with instructions.

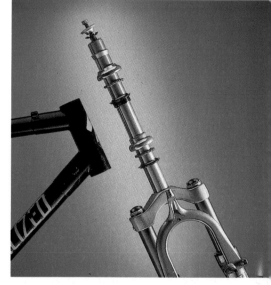

To dismantle the headset, loosen the upper locknut with two headset spanners and then unscrew the headset completely. The forks can then be pulled out from the bottom of the head tube.

When fitting suspension forks, make sure all parts of the headset are positioned correctly. A specialist tool is required to fit the fork race, or it can be knocked carefully into place on the steerer tube with a screwdriver and hammer. Pack all bearings with plenty of grease.

Use a broom handle or another suitable piece of wood to knock the expanding washer into the steerer tube. The washer must sit tightly but not too deeply in the steerer.

After fitting the suspension forks, you will have to replace the brake arms and readjust the brakes. The new headset will also have to be adjusted correctly of course. In order to fit the rubber grips to the handlebars, spray the inside of them with hairspray before attaching them.

Dismantling the forks

The stem is held in place by an expander wedge. First loosen the Allen key bolt that holds the wedge in place. If the stem will not move, a few smart taps with a rubber mallet might help. (The fork race is usually a little rusted and difficult to dislodge from the steerer tube.)

Next, remove the cantilever brakes from the pivot bosses on the fork and take out the old headset. Hold the top cup in place with a headset spanner and loosen the locknut. You will then be able to unscrew both nuts completely and pull the forks out from the bottom of the head tube.

A special tool is needed to remove the old bottom bearing set. This "rocket tool" slips into the head tube and its four flared parts allow you to knock out the headset cups with a hammer. A long, sturdy screwdriver and a hammer can also be used to tap out the bottom bearing set evenly.

A certain degree of skill and intuition is also needed when fixing the fork race on to the new suspension forks. Ask your dealer to machine the steerer tube accurately. There is a special tool for this, but it is too expensive to purchase unless you are going to make a habit of fitting new forks. The fork race (on which the lower headset bearings run) sits at the bottom of the steerer tube and is fitted by means of another special tool that is basically a piece of tubing that fits tightly over the steerer tube like a sleeve. It can also be hammered carefully into place with a screwdriver.

Cutting the forks down

You now need to cut the steerer tube to size. You will need a hacksaw and a vice in which to clamp the tube as you cut it cleanly to the exact length. If your bike already had an Aheadset fitted, simply measure the length of the old steerer tube and cut the new one to the same size. Otherwise, measure the length of the head tube and add the full height of the headset and stem, minus 2 mm (1/8 in) for the top cap on the Aheadset. The simplest way of doing this is to insert the forks with the complete headset into the frame, place the stem on top and mark the upper edge with a felt-tip pen. You can then cut the steerer tube at a point 2 mm (1/8 in) below this mark.

In order to fit the Aheadset, the expanding washer has to be knocked into the steerer. This can be done with a piece of wood, a broom handle or something similar, that will fit inside the steerer. The washer must sit absolutely tightly in the steerer tube, because it holds in place the adjuster bolt in the stem that controls the adjustment of the whole headset.

Fitting the forks

Now assemble the Aheadset parts in the correct order on the steerer (see picture) and fit the stem into the tube. Pack the bearings with plenty of grease. Next fit the control levers on to the handlebars and replace the cantilever brakes on the pivot bosses. It is a good idea to put a little grease on the pivot bosses as well. You may find it easier to fit the grips if you spray a little hair spray on them: they will slide more easily on to the bars and stay in place better.

Once you have fitted the cantilever brakes, they will have to be readjusted (see pp. 20ff.). Adjust the headset as described. (This can now be done with just one Allen key.) Follow the manufacturer's instructions for adjusting or servicing the suspension forks.

Index